Highlights
Hidden Pictures

My First
Lift-the-Flap
HALLOWEEN
Jokes

Kid Tested by
Atticus Rowe
Age 5

HIGHLIGHTS PRESS
Honesdale, Pennsylvania

Find these hidden objects in the scene.

Magnifying Glass · Ice-Cream Bar · Broccoli

Broom · Island · Drinking Straw

Bowl · Paper Airplane · Clipboard

Pickle · Lightning Bolt · Mountain

Happy Owl-o-ween!

Find these hidden objects in the scene.

Teacup — Scarf — Waffle

Flashlight — Kite — Ring

Magnet — Tent — Tooth

Safety Pin — Doughnut — Spoon

With a pumpkin patch

How do you fix a broken jack-o'-lantern?

Find these hidden objects in the scene.

Football · Seashell · Open Book

Slice of Cake · Acorn · Sock

Suitcase · Wristwatch · Heart

Raindrop · Letter · Key

Boo-berries

What is a ghost's favorite fruit?

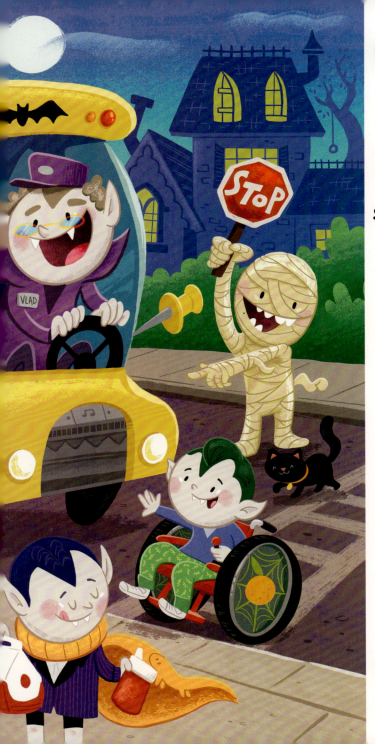

Find these hidden objects in the scene.

Salamander   Pushpin   Orange

Purse   Toothpaste   Rowboat

Fish   Flute   Mop

Harmonica   Pennant   Crown

Their bat-to-school clothes

Find these hidden objects in the scene.

Basketball · Lock · Lollipop

Pineapple · Slice of Bread · Hand

Fork · Rolling Pin · Banana

Sun · Frog · Button

On the tele-bone

Find these hidden objects in the scene.

Mushroom **Bell** **Ball of Yarn**

Envelope **Belt** **Mailbox**

Saw **Knitted Hat** **Skateboard**

Croissant **Cactus** **Wishbone**

Hello, hello, hello!

Find these hidden objects in the scene.

 Pear   Feather   Toaster

 Artist's Brush  Hockey Stick   Wedge of Lemon

 Umbrella   Canoe  Carrot

 Pine Cone   Worm Arrow

Scream cheese

What does a witch put on her bagel?

Find these hidden objects in the scene.

 Saltshaker
 Scissors
 Turtle
 Fishhook
 Ribbon
 Flag
 Necktie
 Spool of Thread
 Slice of Pizza
 Paintbrush
 Peanut
 Needle

He was already stuffed.

Find these hidden objects in the scene.

Horn   **Magnifying Glass**   **Toothbrush**

Sailboat   **Zipper**   **Baseball Bat**

Jack   **Boot**   **Feather**

Flower   **Mug**   **Hamburger**

She was learning a new language.

Find these hidden objects in the scene.

Ladder

Ruler

Snake

Shovel

Ice-Cream Cone

Candle

Boomerang

Hanger

Crayon

Horseshoe

Worm

Yo-Yo

The scary-go-round

What's a ghost's favorite carnival ride?

Find these hidden objects in the scene.

Comb — Pen — Cupcake

Bird — Boot — Mitten

Golf Club — Pineapple — Balloon

Bowling Ball — Vest — Wedge of Cheese

On Chews-day

When do Halloween monsters eat their candy?

Answers